Russian Tortoise Care

Russian Tortoise Pet Owner's Guide

Russian Tortoises General Info, Purchasing, Care, Cost, Keeping, Health, Supplies, Food, and More Included!

By Lolly Brown

Copyrights and Trademarks

All rights reserved. No part of this book may be reproduced or transformed in any form or by any means, graphic, electronic, or mechanical, including photocopying, recording, taping, or by any information storage retrieval system, without the written permission of the author.

This publication is Copyright ©2022 NRB Publishing, an imprint. Nevada. All products, graphics, publications, software and services mentioned and recommended in this publication are protected by trademarks. In such instance, all trademarks & copyright belong to the respective owners. For information consult www.NRBpublishing.com

Disclaimer and Legal Notice

This product is not legal, medical, or accounting advice and should not be interpreted in that manner. You need to do your own due-diligence to determine if the content of this product is right for you. While every attempt has been made to verify the information shared in this publication, neither the author, neither publisher, nor the affiliates assume any responsibility for errors, omissions or contrary interpretation of the subject matter herein. Any perceived slights to any specific person(s) or organization(s) are purely unintentional.

We have no control over the nature, content and availability of the web sites listed in this book. The inclusion of any web site links does not necessarily imply a recommendation or endorse the views expressed within them. We take no responsibility for, and will not be liable for, the websites being temporarily unavailable or being removed from the internet.

The accuracy and completeness of information provided herein and opinions stated herein are not guaranteed or warranted to produce any particular results, and the advice and strategies, contained herein may not be suitable for every individual. Neither the author nor the publisher shall be liable for any loss incurred as a consequence of the use and application, directly or indirectly, of any information presented in this work. This publication is designed to provide information in regard to the subject matter covered.

Neither the author nor the publisher assume any responsibility for any errors or omissions, nor do they represent or warrant that the ideas, information, actions, plans, suggestions contained in this book is in all cases accurate. It is the reader's responsibility to find advice before putting anything written in this book into practice. The information in this book is not intended to serve as legal, medical, or accounting advice.

Foreword

Have you ever passed by a pet store and thought of owning your own pet? Why not take care of a Russian Tortoise?

These little creatures like to burrow and play around their area. Make sure you will give a lot of places for them to hide and play! Do not fret, these creatures will be gentle and behave once you handle them! They have sweet personality that would surely hit home when you take them home.

Aside from this, they have human like attributes, they know the time! They know the 12 hours of darkness coupled with the 12 hours of light.

You will surely know that these creatures are truly a breeze to take care of because they are herbivore. They would eat whatever they can! Well, not meat. This breed is imported from Russia; however, they are bred to be sold so you know that they are priced cheap.

If you ever think of owning your first Russian Tortoise, we will help you! This book will give you all of the information that you would possibly need if you will be a tortoise owner soon enough! Do not be afraid of this journey and let us move on! Happy reading!

Table of Contents

Introduction 1

Chapter One: Biological Information 3

   Where Did They Come From? 4

   How They Got Here 5

   Size, Life Span, and Physical Appearance 6

      Quick Facts 8

Chapter Two: Owning Your Russian Tortoise 11

   The Russian Tortoise as a Pet 12

      Temperament and Behavioral Characteristics 13

   Why Choose Russian Tortoise? 14

   Licensing Requirement for Russian Tortoise ... 16

   Cost of Owning Russian Tortoises 18

   The Necessities 18

      Cost of Russian Tortoises 19

      UV-A and UV-B Light Source 20

      Tank and Tank Stand 20

      Bedding and Substrate 21

      Filtration System and Pump 22

      Humidity and Temperature 23

      Tortoise Food 23

      Vet Consultation 24

Chapter Three: Purchasing Your Russian Tortoises 25
- Where Can I Acquire My Russian Tortoise? 26
- The Reputable and Smart Russian Tortoise Breeder 29
- Characteristics of a Healthy Breed 34

Chapter Four: A Happy Household for Your Russian Tortoises 37
- Housing Requirements 39
- Indoor or Outdoor: Where Should I Put It? 40
    - Indoor Habitat 41
    - Outdoor Habitat 42
    - Cage 46
    - UV & UVB Light 48
    - Night Light 49
    - Substrate 50
- Indoor Enclosures for Hatchlings/ Juveniles 52
- Outdoor Enclosures for Adult Tortoises 53
- Habitat Tips 56
- Habitat Maintenance Tips 58
- The Proper Housing Temperature 59
- Hibernation 60
    - Types of Hibernations 61
- Post - Hibernation 63

Chapter Five: Russian Tortoise's Feeding Guide 65

    A Suitable Diet for My Russian Tortoise 66

    Variation Is the Key 68

    Food You Can Give To Your Russian Tortoise 69

    What Not To Give To My Russian Tortoise: 74

    Supplements: Yay or Nay? 75

    Where Can I Buy Food For My Russian Tortoise? 76

    Online Shops 77

Chapter Six: Proper Hygiene and Grooming For Your Russian Tortoise 81

    Hygiene for Your Russian Tortoise 82

        Grooming 101 82

    Prepare the Materials: 84

        Cleaning Your Russian Tortoise Thoroughly 86

Chapter Seven: Care Sheet and Summary 91

    Glossary 101

Photo Credits 107

References 109

Introduction

Russian Tortoise is also known as the Horsefield's Tortoise. Aside from this, they are also known as the four-toed tortoise, the Afghan, the Steppe, and the central Asian.

These creatures are normally found in rocky deserts in Iran, Russia, Afghanistan, Pakistan, and usually found at very high elevations. In these places, they live in large underground burrows, where they would stay for months during extreme temperature.

They are usually imported in different countries for domestic pet trade. Some are found in pet stores, while some people continually breed them for adoption.

Introduction

They are small but contain big personality. These Russian Tortoises are the breed to watch out for, because they are one of the most popular tortoises that are kept as pets. Although they are slow, these are very active and responsive to their owners. They are branded to be the greatest first reptile that you will ever have.

If you have taken this greatly, and it is very easy, some of these tortoises could live up to 40 years! Are you ready for that long-term relationship?

In this 40 years, you must need a lot of information about the Russian Tortoise. The world is a battlefield and any armory is great. You need to know how to take care of this tortoise, a house to live in, how to handle it, how to groom it, how to feed it, and how to take care of it when it is sick.

You might think it is difficult to know all of these things at once, but, do not worry, we are here to help you!

This book is your go-to guide to any knowledge about the Russian Tortoise. We will give you detailed information on its background, quickest facts possible, and how to take care of this as a pet.

Chapter One: Biological Information

Welcoming a new pet into your life is not an easy task. You need to adjust yourself and your household to this setting. However, before you do all of these things, you need to figure out the pet that you want.

A key to finding the pet that would fit you and your personality knows its background. Knowing the background would give you a sense of "connection" with the pet that you want to acquire.

A Russian Tortoise is a great way for you to have your first pet. A tortoise is a gentle pet that would entertain you for hours.

Chapter One: Biological Information

You would easily find this specie available everywhere, as this is one of the most sought pet in the breeding industry.

Initially, they are only an inch in length but they may reach as long as eight to ten inches long when they mature! A distinguishing feature is that females are larger than male.

Have you ever wondered where this specie came from? Are you curious with the roots of these adorable little reptiles? Do not fret, because we will help you explore where the Russian Tortoise originated and how the specie managed to expand across many regions and countries.

While we are learning history, we will slowly unfold the brilliance of our beloved Russian Tortoise.

This chapter will deal with the origin of our beloved specie.

Where Did They Come From?

Our beloved Russian Tortoise a bite-sized reptile. Their rich history and origin lies within the historical countries of North Pakistan, Afghanistan, and the Soviet Territory Kazakhstan.

These tortoises can also be called the Steppe Tortoise, Afghanistan Tortoise, and even Four-toed Tortoise.

Chapter One: Biological Information

Presently, you can see wild Russian Tortoise in several countries such as Iran, Pakistan, Russia, and China.

If you ever happen to see these tortoises on these countries, it is common because of the dry and sandy landscape within these regions.

The true origin of this Russian Tortoise is classified as Testudo Genus. This specific genus refers to a cluster of different species of tortoise that are known for their extremely small size and their precious history.

How They Got Here

These pet initially began their journey to the United States around the 1970s.

When these initial imports began, many of these tortoises are brought to the United States on an annual basis. Russian Tortoises are considered to be an ideal pet for those who are staying in North America for various reasons.

The amicable nature and convenient size are the main reasons for the introduction of this specie in North America. Soon enough, they have become one of the most popular animal imports coming from Middle Asia.

The total history of this Russian Tortoise is truly intriguing and mysterious. However, due to its intriguing

Chapter One: Biological Information

and mysterious history, they became the chosen import because of this ingenuity and adaptability.

The Russian Tortoise is the perfect animal to import and distribute due to its easy ability to adapt to quickly changing environment and environmental conditions.

You can truly see the popularity of the Russian Tortoise through its widespread expansion and importation around North America and beyond. If you truly observe the anthology of this breed, you can see that they have a rich history.

With the introduction of this breed in the late part of the 20th century, this specie became drastically popular. There have been a lot of changes in pet culture due to the introduction of the Russian Tortoise.

Size, Life Span, and Physical Appearance

A hatchling of this specific specie could measure around one inch in carapace length. When they are starting to mature, they could reach a maximum length of eight to 10 inches.

The female Russian Tortoise is normally larger than males when they reach their maximum size. When the females are around six inches long, they become large enough to produce their own eggs.

Chapter One: Biological Information

Russian tortoise is usually imported to the US as young adults between four and five inches in carapace length. During this phase, the tortoises are large enough to handle extreme conditions during shipping, but small enough to fit in many fixed-size shipping crate.

If you plan on getting a Russian Tortoise with the length of six inches, it will be very difficult to find.

If you raise your Russian Tortoise in a lean, high-fiber diet, captive animal that is found in a low-stress environment, it could live up to 40 years.

The top part of the shell of the Russian Tortoise could be in between of tan, yellow to olive color. Typically, they have brown to black markings.

The bottom of the shell could be a solid black or has pieces or blotches of black or brown. The tip of the tail is very hard and full of bones. In males, the tail is longer and the skin is yellow to tan in color.

A very unique characteristic that makes Russian Tortoise stand out is that they have four claws on each foot, so they are known as the "four-toed tortoise."

Chapter One: Biological Information

Quick Facts

Distribution and Range: The Russian Tortoise came from North Pakistan, Afghanistan, and the Soviet Territory Kazakhstan. However, they are scattered throughout North America and its neighboring region.

Breed Size: small size

Body Type and Appearance:

Length: typically, the Russian Tortoise ranges from 13-25 cm or 5-10 in. The females grow from 15-25 cm or 6-10 in, while the male averages from 13 to 20 cm or 5 to 8 inches.

Skin Texture: the texture is rough, sculpted shell

Color: colors may vary, but its outer shell is typically black or ruddy brown. Between the scutes, the colors may fade to yellow. The tortoise's body could be brown or straw-yellow.

Temperament: We can describe the Russian Tortoise as amicable, open, and vibrant. They also have friendly nature.

Diet: The diet of the Russian Tortoise is generally herbivores. They love to eat and prefer leafy greens. This specie need to consume a high fiber diet. This should consist of hay, greens such as kale, collards, turnip, dandelion greens, mustard, dark lettuce, various vegetables such as corn, squash, carrots, peppers, sweet potatoes, and prickly pear cactus. They could also consume a small amount of

Chapter One: Biological Information

fruit such as berries and apple. However, you should not feed your Tortoise nutrient deficient food such as grains, iceberg lettuce, or meat.

Habitat: When the climate permits, you should house your Russian Tortoise outside of your home in large, penned-off areas that your frog could have an easy access to safe plants such as cassia, prickly pear, morning glory, and various grasses.

Health Condition: Russian Tortoises are hardy reptiles. However, they can still suffer from gastrointestinal (GI) parasite that would cause weight loss and diarrhea; this parasite is transmittable to humans. Other than that, Russian Tortoise may carry the Salmonella bacteria.

Life Span: forty years in captivity if you have kept it in great condition, such as giving good food and environment to live in.

These are just some essential information that you need to remember about the Russian Tortoise. This information is important because you will be constantly taking care of your tortoise for a long time. This is a long time commitment and you really need to commit yourself from the very start.

However, there are still a lot of things you need to know, to do, and to prepare before you go out and buy your Russian Tortoise. Taking care of a pet is a big task; this book

Chapter One: Biological Information

will help you with know the essentials. You need to provide a great environment for the pet so it can have a happy and healthy life. You need to provide its initial needs.

Before you go out and buy your very first Russian Tortoise, you need to give the Tortoise its initial need. Before you fully make up your decision, make sure that you read more about this lovely and caring creature.

Aside from the things you need to prepare, this book will give you the health considerations, substrate requirements, feeding requirements, as well as proper handling. Make sure that you thoroughly read this book before you decide to own your first pet. Enjoy the tips and how - tos!

Chapter Two: Owning Your Russian Tortoise

We have already discussed the essential information and history about the Russian Tortoise. We believe that you have possessed great deal of knowledge on its history. From this point forward, we will be discussing your Russian Tortoise as a pet. This will help you to decide whether you would really own this specie of Tortoise.

In this chapter, we will dig deeper on its behavioral traits, licenses and permits to keep them legally, and a budget to provide all of its need.

Chapter Two: Owning Your Russian Tortoise

Before you go out and purchase your own Russian Tortoise, you need to remember to buy these things to provide a happy life for your lovely creature. Let us read on and know the magical world of the Russian Tortoise.

The Russian Tortoise as a Pet

Deciding to have a pet is a very big decision. Your whole life will change as you need to put in your heart and soul to take care of another creature. Remember that you will be keeping this tortoise as a pet so you need to responsible for its well-being, as well as its natural habitat.

Having a Russian Tortoise is an enjoyable experience, especially for both seasoned and even new reptile owners. This specie will become the best roommate that you will have! Your Russian Tortoise is very easy to handle, it is always welcoming, low maintenance, and very cute to handle!

They have a natural knack for adventure and they can easily adapt to the outdoor and indoor living situation. Aside from this, they can adjust well to different house living condition.

Chapter Two: Owning Your Russian Tortoise

Temperament and Behavioral Characteristics

We can describe the Russian Tortoise as active, friendly, and outgoing.

If you are first time reptile parents, you might become scared on handling it. However, they will become gentle once you learn how to handle them gentle, and throughout time.

Aside from this, you need to move slowly around them so you won't startle them. This specie is very adept at digging for escape as well as hides in different objects and burrow into their substrate.

Generally, your Russian Tortoise would remain dormant during winter and become active during summer time. They do not really like to be indoors, instead, they thrive better when they are kept in open habitats.

During summer, they like to burrow but comes out of hiding when the sun goes down. This specie is a social animal and they often enter when there is a burrow. Sometimes, you can see a lot of Russian Tortoises spend time in one burrow.

Further, they are considered as terrestrial animals and can thrive in dry environments such as dry mountainous regions and deserts.

Chapter Two: Owning Your Russian Tortoise

Just like any animal, you need to keep in mind that your Russian Tortoise will take time to get use to different environment, so if you see that they are a little shy, do not fret, because they need to just adjust and get warmed up to you.

Why Choose Russian Tortoise?

Some people like keeping pets like their home companions, while some may be selective on which kind of pet they will get. There are a lot of pet you can choose from, also, there are a lot of factors such as type of care and housing requirement you need to provide.

In this part, we will go in detail on why or why not you should get a Russian Tortoise. Consider each points because this will help you make up your mind in getting your first Russian Tortoise.

Why I Want a Russian Tortoise

- You can easily find this at different pet stores as they are one of the most common reptiles that you can get.

- You can easily find information about Russian Tortoise everywhere.

Chapter Two: Owning Your Russian Tortoise

- They can live on for hundreds of years, if taken care of.

- They are great for first time reptile owners.

- They hibernate for long times, so you do not need to worry about its everyday needs.

- You do not need to interact with the tortoise at all times, sometimes they will just interact when you need to feed it.

Why I Don't Want to Own a Russian Tortoise

- They need to have certain temperature at all times to live.

- They do not do well indoors. They like to play around and burrow in their preferred hiding spots.

- You may need to provide proper lighting sources at home.

- You need to give a diet specific for your Russian Tortoise, so it can get all the proper minerals and vitamins.

Chapter Two: Owning Your Russian Tortoise

- You need to constantly provide clean water on a daily basis. The Russian Tortoise needs to be soaked in water at least once or twice a week.

- You might need an assistance if you are planning to travel and leave your pet behind.

These are just some considerations that you need to think if you of getting your own Russian Tortoise. However, you need to remember that all pets are difficult to take care of. You will exert time and effort in any pet that you would choose.

If you still have your mind set in getting a Russian Tortoise, even after going through the list, let us continue reading to know more about this pet. In the succeeding parts, you will know the future costs and licenses if you ever want to purchase them as pet.

Licensing Requirement for Russian Tortoise

If you want to own a Russian Tortoise, you need to comply with the rules and regulation before you go out and buy it. The license and requirements are there to protect both you and your pet wherever you may be.

Chapter Two: Owning Your Russian Tortoise

A specific organization, namely Convention on International Trade in Endangered Species (CITES), is responsible for taking care of all animals - especially those who are endangered.

Latin America, USA, Asia, Europe, and Australia are some of the CITE member countries. You need to provide all the proper and legal documents about the animal that you want to keep as your own pet, so you would not have future troubles whether at home or if you are travelling.

In this specific organization, there are appendices for different species belonging to different categories. In these categories, there are different ruling for keeping, exporting, and trading your Russian Tortoise.

You can't travel with your Russian Tortoise abroad if you do not possess all the certificates coming from CITES both from the country of origin and the country of destination.

These certificates will be brought to authorities to prove that you have bought the Russian Tortoise safely and legally.

Prepare document such as your pet's name, identity, and characteristics. The document should also contain your name, address, and any basic information deemed necessary. Although you do not really need to ask approval

Chapter Two: Owning Your Russian Tortoise

from any organization or authority, you just need to prepare these for future reference.

Cost of Owning Russian Tortoises

If you plan to own a Russian Tortoise, you know that you need to provide a lot of things for this creature. They are just not like your typical dogs or cats that you can squeeze into your life. You need to think of the source of the Russian Tortoise, the aquarium or any open space that your Tortoise could use as a home, food bowls, water dishes, different bulbs for heat sources, reptile humidifier, and food supplies and supplements.

If you believe you can handle these things, let us go ahead and read on the succeeding chapters!

The Necessities

Having a pet in your life is not easy. Before purchasing your pet, you need to plan out everything and prepare yourself, your family, and your house for the big change that will happen. Bringing a pet into your home is just like bringing your child into the world. You need to give shelter, water, food, and other basic necessities. Aside from

Chapter Two: Owning Your Russian Tortoise

this, you need to set aside a budget for your pet.

Creating a new budget for your pet might be difficult at first, but you will surely get a hang of it in the future.

The cost of all your expenses will depend on different factors, such as the type and kind of resources that you will buy. In some cases, items might be priced higher due to their limited stocks. Remember to keep in mind the quality and longevity of the product that you will buy. The items might be cheap, but if they are not of good quality - you should not buy that.

In this part, we will give you a breakdown of the things you need to ready when you have a Russian Tortoise.

Cost of Russian Tortoises

The price of the Russian Tortoise would depend on the size, gender, and age that you would buy. Make sure that you already know what kind of tortoise you would buy.

A hatchling's price could shoot up to $225. An adult female could be priced up $149 to $249.

Find a reputable breeder to ensure that you get the best tortoise as possible.

Chapter Two: Owning Your Russian Tortoise

Other Essentials

Having a Russian Tortoise in your life is slightly difficult. You need to set aside a specific budget for all the essentials that you will purchase.

Some of these things are only one time thing while some are recurrent expenses. Make sure that you get the best kind of essential for your Russian Tortoise. Also, make sure that you have a back-up in case your equipment will be broken.

UV-A and UV-B Light Source

Your aquarium filters out the UV rays needed by your tortoise to be healthy. If you plan to have your tortoise at home, you need to have an artificial light source with UV-B tube fluorescent together with UV-A producing basking bulbs.

UV-B bulbs are typically $20 up to $40, while UV-A bulbs range from $10 to $20.

Tank and Tank Stand

You need around ten gallons of tank for every inch of your tortoise's shell. Your Russian Tortoise prefers to have an outdoor enclosure, especially during warmer client. A room for one or two adults should be more than 2 feet by 4

Chapter Two: Owning Your Russian Tortoise

feet.

The walls should be around six to 12 inches from the ground; this is to prevent your tortoise to dig from the side. Aside from it, it should be 12 inches or higher above the ground.

Russian Tortoises are natural burrowers. They love to dig into corners and against almost any object! You need to put large rocks under the soil to prevent your pet from ever digging out. The tank is around $200.

Bedding and Substrate

If you are building a habitat for your Russian Tortoise, you need to think of where you will place your pet. In any situation that you will choose, you need to have a bedding material that will serve as your tortoise's footing and temperature regulation. Some of the substrate could include:

- Grass
- Alfafa
- Timothy Hay
- Sand
- Gravel
- Cypress Mulch
- Hay
- Wood Chips

Chapter Two: Owning Your Russian Tortoise

- Soil
- Pine Bark Mulch
- Aspen Bedding

It may be your personal choice, but you can mix several types of bedding together rather than just picking one.

Any of these things can be easily bought at a pet store, landscaping supplier or a retailer for home improvement.

In some cases, if you buy from a professional establishment, it could ensure a high quality of a product. However, you could also find the supplies in nature, but be careful in getting this from nature, because the bedding could contain: contamination of materials, chemicals, pesticides, and debris. This will cost anywhere from $20 to $30 or more.

Filtration System and Pump

Tortoises are pretty messy creatures, especially your Russian Tortoise that likes to burrow and hide. In this light, you need to have filter that is twice the size of your tank. Even if you have a great filter system, you need to clean your tank and change the water frequently. A good filter

Chapter Two: Owning Your Russian Tortoise

system starts at $70.

Humidity and Temperature

The basking are should be the warmest area in the cage. It should be around 90 to 95 degrees. You can put ceramic emitters and under tank heaters. The humidity should not be higher than 60%. However, humidity is not really that important to Russian Tortoise because they are easily adaptable. But remember that Russian Tortoise has little tolerance for cold, humid, or wet conditions.

If they have constantly exposure to these things, it could lead to a number of health issues such as shell rot, pneumonia, and eye infection.

Tortoise Food

Just like humans, you need to give a variety of food for your pet's diet. Your Russian Tortoise is herbivores in their nature. The diet should have a variety of leafy, dark, greens. Aside from this, you could also add squash, carrots, and bell peppers. You could also give figs, bananas, apple, and strawberries, but only as a treat. However, these fruits should not be more than 10% of the animal's diet. Typically, your budget would run from $45 and up.

Chapter Two: Owning Your Russian Tortoise

Vet Consultation

In some cases, your pet will get sick. It is best to set aside a rainy day fund in case your pet will get sick. Make sure to set aside a budget of around $50 and up for any medical needs.

In summary, these are the essential things that you need to remember when getting your Russian Tortoise. By now, you should have made up your mind on whether or not you will buy your Russian Tortoise.

Be prepared for the wild journey ahead because we will be exploring more about our beloved pet.

Chapter Three: Purchasing Your Russian Tortoises

In this part, we will give you a run down on the things you need to see about your Russian Tortoise. Aside from this, we will also help you spot the best and reputable breeder in your area. We will also be giving you different places where you can buy your Russian Tortoises.

In purchasing your pet, you need to primarily now the background of both the pet and breeder and how s/he raised it. In some scenarios, you could also acquire your Russian Tortoise in the internet and these sites could also help you in your journey as a reptile owner. Buying healthy species is the key to have a happy and healthy tortoise in the

Chapter Three: Purchasing Your Russian Tortoises

future. If you have chosen the correct specie, you would have a time of your life when you are taking care of it.

Where Can I Acquire My Russian Tortoise?

In this part, we will be giving you place where you can purchase your own Russian tortoise and how to spot if the seller is selling it legally or illegally.

There are a lot of choices in this section, thus, we will be providing you with the pros and cons so you can choose the best choice possible.

Keep an open mind with all of these choices easily available to you, find on that are easily convenient to you and would present you with the best result possible. But, you can also ask around and seek advice from professionals and friends. You can also ask other reptile owners who their preferred seller is. A trustworthy referral is better than a ton of reviews.

Local Pet Stores/ Concept Stores

This is the first choice for many people. People who prefer this path are those who do not have enough time to search for the right place to buy your first pet.

Chapter Three: Purchasing Your Russian Tortoises

You just need to go to your nearest pet store and select the healthiest Russian Tortoise.

People like this option because it is very accessible for many areas and this is for people who have little to no time in seeking a right place. However, some stores might not carry the breed of choice. Aside from that, you could not really know the background knowledge about the specie that you would want. And, you still need to drive to the nearest pet store to buy your pet. Remember, some pet stores are just 'production' sites, which means that they do not really care for the quality of the species, they just want to have the highest number of specie as possible.

Backyard/Private Owners

Backyard owners are those who breed their own Russian Tortoise. If you have already bought a pet, you might know the process on how this goes.

Some people prefer this option because they can truly know the breeder of the specie that they want. They would know how background of both the parents and the tortoise itself. Aside from that, you can ask the breeder several questions about the chosen specie, you can ask how to take care of it and housing requirements.

If both you and the breeder are friendly, you can even haggle the price of the chosen tortoise. You can know the

Chapter Three: Purchasing Your Russian Tortoises

real characteristics of the tortoise through talking to the owner. However, you might have a difficult time in searching for the best owner possible. You might need to ask for referrals from your family and friends, and you should not immediately settle down on the first breeder of your choosing. Other than that, you need to drive up to the specific breeding spots to thoroughly inspect the place and the specie that you are looking for.

Some owners might even 'scam' you for money. If you do not know what questions to ask and what things to look for, you will be very easily fooled by the first person you see.

You can also know backyard breeders through conventions and even vets. They might know other people who own the specific specie that you want.

Online Stores

The internet age is upon us. It has given us a channel of endless possibilities. Further, it has given us online stores which ease our way on finding the thing that we want to buy.

You just need to browse different sites to know the best deal possible. Because we live in the digital, you can search on your laptops, smart phones and tablets! No one is stopping you from browsing a Russian Tortoise from your

Chapter Three: Purchasing Your Russian Tortoises

bathroom! In some stores, they may even offer you delivery. If you can't drive up to the location, the Russian Tortoise will be given to you! However, you can't really know the characteristic of the parent and the specific specie until they have given it to you. You might get scammed if you buy from sites that are not really verified.

If you want to continue doing this way, you might need to seek advice from your family and even friends, especially if they have bought from this location before.

The Reputable and Smart Russian Tortoise Breeder

Finding the right person to buy your Russian Tortoise from is very difficult. You need to do an extensive process before you even decide which breeder to choose.

First, you need to look for the breeder who is caring, responsible and reputable. Some might consider themselves as "reputable," but there are tell - tale signs for you to know before you contact the people.

To know if the person you are looking for is a great breeder, you need to ask the correct questions about the specie that they are selling. Remember, you need to give the correct answers for you. If you are not satisfied with the answer that they have given you, go out and look for another breeder in your area.

Chapter Three: Purchasing Your Russian Tortoises

Some breeders only raise up their specie because of money and not for health purposes. If you have encountered this person, run out the door because you do not need them in your life. Find someone who is in it to produce next generation of your chosen specie, and not just for the money. If the person you are talking to only knows the basic information and can't answer the important questions - she or he is definitely not a breeder.

Aside from that, the person should also know the housing requirements, feeding guidelines, breeding, and even the health concerns by heart. From that, the breeder should also give you tips on how to handle the pet easily.

In some scenarios, you can find a respectable breeder from networks. Search from Russian Tortoise groups or even your vets. Sometimes an advice weighs deeper than a thorough internet search.

In this portion, we will also give you some guidelines in finding the best breeder for the Russian Tortoise easily.

- **Seek advice.** Ask your friends, relatives, and family members if they know any Russian Tortoise breeder. This might be the best option possible for you. If not, you can go out and search for Russian Tortoise groups.

Chapter Three: Purchasing Your Russian Tortoises

- **Research.** Join online forums and talk to other reptile enthusiasts and ask for their opinion. Sometimes experience is the best teacher in this instance.

- **Further research.** Seek for sites about Russian Tortoise. Sometimes, they link up several sites for you to look at.

- **Weed out the bad stuff.** If the website does not offer enough information that you need, just like the specie, breed, or facilities, cross it off your list.

- **Fact Check.** Make sure that you check the accuracy of the data and the website itself. Some might be bogus sites that would just scam you out of your money. If you see just even a little red flag - get out of there and cross it off your list!

- **Cross it off!** If the breeder does not answer your questions in the way that you want, cross it off. Cross everyone off until you have gotten a handful of breeders that you are sure of. It does not hurt to fact check your breeders.

- **Watch for Red Flags.** If you see that the breeding facility is dirty, cramped up with too much Russian Tortoise - remove it from your list! These are just

Chapter Three: Purchasing Your Russian Tortoises

some red flags that will state that your breeder is just in it for the money.

- **Have human interaction.** You need to contact each breeder individually. You need to know them as well as their personal knowledge of the Russian Tortoise. You should ask specific information concerning the pet of your choice. If you sense that he is up to something, go out of the breeding site immediately!

- **Answer back.** A reputable breeder would also ask you questions about yourself. A breeder would also want to know where his or her tortoises are going. Aside from this, the breeder would also make sure if you are capable of taking care of the specie. Some might even ask to see your house as to see if it is a suitable habitat for the pet.

- **Give it time.** Allot time to going through every detail. Although it might be tiring, you will be ensured that the tortoise you would be getting is of great quality. Do not hesitate to go over the list again if you are not satisfied with the results.

- **Still undecided?** It is okay if you are still undecided on where you will get your Russian Tortoise. It is

Chapter Three: Purchasing Your Russian Tortoises

better to take time knowing the breeder now rather than having troubles with the tortoise in the future.

Questions to Ask

If you will go out and meet your breeder, it is best to be prepared with the questions about the Russian Tortoise. Here are some questions that you can ask the breeder. You can use these questions and add your own for your own protection,

- What other information can you tell me about the Russian Tortoise?

- What feeding instruction would you recommend? Is there a special diet that I need to follow for this specific specie?

- How can I give it a sustainable habitat? What brands would you recommend for its substrate? Should I let it stay inside or outside?

- How would I breed my Russian Tortoise? How did you raise this specific batch?

Chapter Three: Purchasing Your Russian Tortoises

- Where is the preferred place for the habitat? What should be the correct temperature? How should I set up the half-and-half tank?

- How many years have you been breeding the tortoise? What kind of experience do you have?

- Do you breed other species of tortoises? Or do you just specialize in Russian Tortoise?

- Can you offer me a warranty or guarantee? For how long?

- Can I ask any referrals for vets, food brands, supplies, and etc.?

Characteristics of a Healthy Breed

The age, gender, and size are totally up to you. However, there are still several characteristics you need to remember to have the best specie as possible. Here are some of the things you need to look for in a healthy species:

✓ Your tortoise should have clear eyes, clean nose, and clean bum.

✓ There should not be any signs of shell damage.

Chapter Three: Purchasing Your Russian Tortoises

- ✓ The Russian Tortoise should be active or alert at all times.
- ✓ The tortoise should feel strong and heavy.

There are things that you still need to avoid, such as:

- ❖ Cloudy eyes
- ❖ There is a mucus build - up in the nose
- ❖ There is a residue on the bum
- ❖ There is a visual damage on the shell, or "pyramiding"
- ❖ The tortoise is incoherent or non-responsive
- ❖ If you feel that the Russian Tortoise is weak or light.
- ❖ If the breeding area is too crowded with different kinds of tortoises.

These are the things that you need to remember when purchasing your very first Russian Tortoise. Do not be afraid to seek help from your family and friends as they might know better than you. Aside from that, it is best to still search the internet on the several sites you can buy a Russian Tortoise.

In the succeeding chapter, we will be welcoming your Russian Tortoise in your home.

Chapter Three: Purchasing Your Russian Tortoises

Chapter Four: A Happy Household for Your Russian Tortoises

You have now decided that you want a Russian Tortoise in your life. This book has given you a lot of information that you need about the specific specie.

Aside from that, you now know where to get great specie, as well as spotting a great kind. We hope that you will use this in your future endeavor. However, your job is not yet done. Before bringing your Russian Tortoise at home, you must set up the habitat requirements as well the caging needs of your pet. This should come first before the diet, handling, and even breeding the pet.

Chapter Four: Happy Household for Your Russian Tortoises

A conducive environment would mimic the natural habitat of your Russian Tortoise. You would use the necessary housing needs, materials, and give your pet a happy life. This would prevent your pet from being stressed out.

Before you even buy your Russian Tortoise, you should have already set up your home for your first reptile. If you bought your pet first, you might have a difficult time in both taking care of the pet and setting up the cage. Remember, this tortoise like to burrow and hide - you would not want to play hide and seek with your pet!

You need a lot of materials to set-up a happy home but do not fret, you have a lot places to buy from! But them early before your time runs out.

In this section, we will give you the habitat requirements as well as setting up a suitable cage for the Russian Tortoise. You might need to decide where to keep your pet, inside or outside? Look out in your area and make sure you put it on a cozy place.

Chapter Four: Happy Household for Your Russian Tortoises

Housing Requirements

These are just some of the things needed by your Russian Tortoise to have a happy life:

- Cage
- Light
- Night Light
- Substrate
- Humidifier
- Terrarium

Your Russian Tortoise is a reptile which means it has a special environment to live in, especially to adapt to its need.

Your Russian Tortoise needs to have a fairly dry environment, however, it may need the occasion soak in water. In colder climate, they also hibernate or aestivate and they need a space where they could retreat and hide from too much heat or too much cold.

Aside from this, do not forget that your Russian Tortoise is very active and they might escape through climbing or digging through their enclosure.

Your enclosure should be high enough to defeat your pet's need from ever climbing up. Aside from this, the

Chapter Four: Happy Household for Your Russian Tortoises

substrate should be more than 12 inches deep; this is to prevent the Russian Tortoise from hitting the ground and hurting itself.

Your Russian Tortoise is really appreciative. You should put living and non-living objects within their sight; some things that you could put are herbs, piles of stones, or logs. You can even put large objects as they like to move around and hide in these!

These are some of the needed materials you should purchase and build inside your home. You might think it is expensive, but your pet would surely benefit from these things.

Make sure you ask your breeder and your vet on the best brand for your Russian Tortoise. This would give you the best choice possible.

Indoor or Outdoor: Where Should I Put It?

Russian Tortoises are creatures who are very active. They like to play around and hide on their places. However, they also like to hide and burrow themselves during cold or hot times.

In this essence, you have a choice on what kind of habitat you can give to your pet. In this portion, we will give you the pros and cons of each type of home.

Chapter Four: Happy Household for Your Russian Tortoises

Indoor Habitat

Indoor habitat is primarily put inside your house. You could set up a small space in your living room area where you could keep a pet. However, you pet would not get enough ventilation from this kind of habitat. Aside from this, you need a lot of substrate to fulfill its need. It is also quite a bothersome experience every time you need to clean the tank.

If you are a previous reptile owner, you already know the drill. Here are just some things that you need to prepare:

- substrate
- cleaning materials
- reserve tank for breeding purposes
- reserve tank for cleaning purposes
- reserve tank for quarantine

Some Tips:

- Half garden loam and half sand is ideal for your Russian Tortoise, however, it is difficult for some pet owners to find. In lieu of the garden loam, you can use coconut coir. You can mix the coir with the sand to create the substrate that you prefer.

Chapter Four: Happy Household for Your Russian Tortoises

- Do not use play sand as it will be too dry for your pet.

- If you are planning to have an indoor habitat, the substrate should be purchased not gathered in your garden. Many owners prefer to look around and just gather some stuff that they think is right for tortoise. However, only little natural stuff is okay for the pet. Getting things from the natural element could expose your tortoise from chemicals and harmful parasites.

- Aside from this, if you get substrate from natural sources, they could eat excrement from other animals, which will put your animal in grave danger. You should be very careful in purchasing your substrate for your Russian Tortoise.

Outdoor Habitat

Some species of tortoise needs a sizable enclosure and some might not even like to stay indoors when they mature. For these reasons, your Russian Tortoise design and utilize habitats that we found outdoors.

Outdoor housing will also offer your tortoise to have a natural, unfiltered light as well as fresh air. It will also give the tortoise a chance to graze on weeds and organic plants.

Chapter Four: Happy Household for Your Russian Tortoises

If you are planning to have an outdoor habitat, you should choose a place that is relatively dry. It should not be too damp to be your Russian Tortoise's habitat. It could be a combination of sand and garden loam.

It is very difficult to control the moisture of the outdoor environment. You need to always monitor your Russian Tortoise's substrate outdoor. You should have a ground covering the right substrate material.

If you are planning to have an outdoor habitat, here are some guidelines:

✓ **Species of the Tortoise**

Large species would go well outside but may cause destruction to your property. However, smaller species are more nice however could overheat quickly than the bigger kind. Luckily, our Russian Tortoise can handle different weathers well.

✓ **Size and Age**

Young tortoises should never be found outdoors, you should raise your youngsters inside the house to have a controlled condition until they reach a certain age to take care of itself.

Chapter Four: Happy Household for Your Russian Tortoises

You can slowly teach your tortoise to stay outdoors through slowly transition itself to the outdoors. You can try out one nice day for your tortoise to stay outside then you try for a few days in a row. After the event, make sure you monitor your Russian Tortoise's behavior and health to ensure that there is no adverse effect on the pet.

✓ **Security**

For indoor habitats, you can be sure that your pet will not run off mistakenly. There is no exact consequence for this kind of habitat.

Russian Tortoises are active little burrowers and diggers, they like to dig and hide into their substrate when they have time. Your tortoise could mistakenly escape your house through occasional digging.

To prevent your Russian Tortoise from escaping, you should build an enclosure directly on the ground. The fences or walls should be buried more than a food. Some experts say that you should use a sold floor or mesh.

The walls should also be high enough to prevent your animal from climbing out. A group of tortoise is not actually an expert climber. However, they could create a scaling chain-link that would lead them to escape.

Chapter Four: Happy Household for Your Russian Tortoises

Aside from that, the material used in your wall should not be enticing to your tortoise. Use a smooth surface that would make it difficult for your Russian Tortoise to climb out.

Further, you should keep other animals in the enclosure. Some animals would be birds, dogs, raccoon and even cats. Big species are not really a treat. However, little tortoises could be easily taken away by your hungry cat or a wild opossum. You can use a top for an enclosure. Some tops could be hardware cloth, or chain-link that would allow light to still pass through.

✓ **Houses**

Even though your Russian Tortoise likes outside you should still give a protected and heated shelter to its outdoor habitat. You can modify your old dog's house or even a plywood box.

You can emit heat through ceramic heat emitters or heavy duty pig blankets. The standard temperature should only be around 80 degrees. Also, add a fluffy layer of hay to become insulation, just make sure that there are no fire hazards posed in the area.

Even though you have bought a fancy heated shelter, this would not ensure that your tortoise would sleep here.

Chapter Four: Happy Household for Your Russian Tortoises

You should manually place your animal on the space on the nightly basis until it get used to the idea of staying in the shelter.

You might think there is a lot of work to do in keeping your beloved Russian Tortoise outside. However, it is easier than it looks like! If you decide to go through this path, make sure you thoroughly research the ways on how to set-up an outdoor habitat.

We have now discussed the pros and cons of both the indoor and the outdoor habitat. It is totally up to you to decide on what kind of habitat you would provide. You can experiment with both of the set-up to figure out what kind of environment you can give to your Russian Tortoise.

In this section, we will be sharing with you the essential things to provide to create a happy habitat. These are just some primary resources; you might need to provide more.

Cage

Some Russian Tortoise would end up in great stress if they are not given enough space to play and burrow it. Most of the sunny days, they would want to munch on leaves and even hide behind rocks.

Chapter Four: Happy Household for Your Russian Tortoises

In this essence, you need to provide a space that is big enough for your pet to play and walk around in. This would help them to have good health and happy mindset.

Your hatchlings could be raised in the aquariums, but your adults should be given a new enclosure to live in. You could also provide a space in your garden for it to grow on in. If you are planning to have it inside your house, make a shallow water pool and substrate for the Russian Tortoise to be in. Make sure that you provide scenery that could mimic their natural environment.

Aquariums are a plus, but you could also work with tubs, plastic containers for your Russian Tortoise. You just need a transparent casing so you can easily spot your pet tortoise when it is playing inside.

If you are planning to let it stay outside, you may need to invest in plywood box to serve as a 'night' room for it to sleep in. You can let your Russian Tortoise free during the day and let it explore your garden.

If you are handy, you could DIY your own terrarium or your outside habitat. This is an exhausting yet happy activity for you and your family. This could also be a great way to express your love for your pet.

Chapter Four: Happy Household for Your Russian Tortoises

UV & UVB Light

You should give a balance of UV-A and UV-B lighting to your pet. These two lightings are crucial to keep at healthy dose of climate, nutrition and psychology of your pet. However, UV-C lighting is very dangerous for the Russian Tortoise; this could cause eye damage and skin cancer. Since Russian Tortoises are purely herbivores, they can't really get vitamin D3 from their foods. They need to have either a direct contact with the sunlight or the UV-B light which is also essential for indoors.

If there is an inadequate amount of vitamin D3, it could spur out Metabolic Bone Disease (MBD) which is one of the primary killers of captive turtles and tortoises. You can aide it with supplements; however, too much Vitamin D3 is very toxic.

A typical lighting set-up for your Russian Tortoise is a UV-B light, which is mostly fluorescent, and UV-A lights that should be halogen, mercury vapor, or incandescent. The UV-A light is used as basking lights for your Russian Tortoise.

You need to have a specific measurement, spacing, angle, and distance for the lights. The habitat should have a minor space without any fixtures.

Any reflectors behind the bulbs would increase the output of your light. You need to secure the lights very well;

Chapter Four: Happy Household for Your Russian Tortoises

any movements could potentially freeze or burn your Russian Tortoise to death.

For you, you should not directly look at these lights. These light are very bright and could potentially hurt your eyes and even blind you if you stare long enough.

The UV-A light is needed to regulate your Russian Tortoise's mood, breeding, activity, and mating level. This light is important for your tortoise as they will help them see all the lights needed around them. They could also identify the same species from afar.

Provide these lights in advance and even keep a back-up to ensure that you can provide a steady light source for your pet.

Night Light

UV-A and UV-B lights are typically used for day time. However, your Russian Tortoise still needs its light during the night. Night lights are used by the tortoise to aide their vision without emitting too much light.

Aside from being a light source, the night light will provide you with heat which your Russian Tortoise needs for hatchling tortoises.

Chapter Four: Happy Household for Your Russian Tortoises

In reality, your pet does not really mind what color you will choose, as long as it is strong enough to give heat as well as to guide them through their habitat during the night.

Substrate

There are a lot of talks on what kind of product you need to have to create a healthy substrate for your Russian Tortoise. For some owners, they like to mix sand and garden soil as well as the mixture of peat moss.

The substrate of your choosing should be very deep for your pet to burrow. It should be ten inches deep up to even three feet. Aside from that, your Russian Tortoise needs humidity, so make sure that the substrate of your choosing will not become too moldy.

In choosing the substrate, make sure that these things will not become too wet. It should be enough to mimic their natural surroundings. The ground that contains too much moisture could potentially lead to shell problems.

Some substrates that you can use are:

- Grass
- Alfafa
- Hay (like timothy)
- Wood chips

Chapter Four: Happy Household for Your Russian Tortoises

- Sand
- Soil
- Gravel
- Pine bark mulch
- Cypress mulch
- Aspen bedding

To get the best from these substrates, you can mix a few of these together. You can easily buy a substrate in pet stores, concept stores, and even landscaping stores. Do not get too much from your natural environment. Sand from your garden may contain parasites that are harmful for your pet. When choosing your substrate you should also consider the placement of your habitat:

Humidifier

Your Russian Tortoise needs humidifier to keep it moistened especially during dry season. You can either buy a manual mister which you can use to mist your pet at an interval. However, there are automatic misters in which you could set-up a timer.

Chapter Four: Happy Household for Your Russian Tortoises

Terrarium or Enclosures

In many places in the United States, you can keep your Russian Tortoise in an outside set-up all times of the year. In some cases, you can only put your Russian Tortoise on warmer months, not colder months. We will help you set-up both the indoor and outdoor enclosure for your Russian Tortoise.

Indoor Enclosures for Hatchlings/ Juveniles

Indoor enclosures are primarily used for hatchlings and juveniles. In colder parts of the countries, you can also keep your Russian Tortoise in here where it is too cold for it to stay outside.

Your terrarium could be made from plastic or glass. However, glass would provide you difficulty in maintaining the proper humidity for the Russian Tortoise.

In some cases, your Russian Tortoise would even walk through the glass enclosure because they do not understand the notion of glass in their lives. If you still want to invest in glass terrarium, you need to paint or tape around the bottom around 5" to 6" of the whole enclosure.

Chapter Four: Happy Household for Your Russian Tortoises

The size of your terrarium should always be proportional to the size of your Russian Tortoise. The ratio of the enclosure and the tortoise should be 10 times as long as the length and 5 times as wide as the wide and 3 times as high as its length. In minimum, the size should be around 2 feet by 4 feet.

If you have a 50 gallon clear plastic storage, this would work well. If you start with small terrarium at first, you will need to provide a bigger terrarium for your pet in the long run.

Outdoor Enclosures for Adult Tortoises

In your outside habitat, it should also be large. The maintaining temperature should be around 40 degrees F or even higher. The enclosure should be around 6 feet by 10 feet for one to six tortoises.

Russian Tortoises are natural burrowers, so the walls of your enclosure should be around 8" to 10" underground. The height should also be at least 16 inches. You need to place the enclosure in an area where it could get a lot of sun, a place where it is dry with good drainage during rainy season.

Chapter Four: Happy Household for Your Russian Tortoises

Even if you plan to set-up an indoor habitat, you could still set-up an outdoor playground. You could place your Russian Tortoise in this place for three hours a day, especially during warmer months, and it will surely have great health benefits for your pet.

Landscaping and Cage Accessories

You need to prepare a lot of things for your Russian Tortoise's enclosure. A shallow water dish should be placed on one end to make sure that your tortoise has a place to soak in. The dish should be deep enough for it to wet the shell, but not deep enough for the tortoise to drown.

You can also provide a hide box in the cooler part of the enclosure, preferably away from the basking area. This hiding box needs to be steady. You do not know that your Russian Tortoise could potentially destruct the flimsy designs and decorations around them. You could also put wooden boxes and half logs.

Other than that, you could also put rocks, tunnels, and logs for your Russian Tortoise to climb on, in, and under. However, take caution in placing the decoration. You do to want to clutter your terrarium too much. You need to give your Russian Tortoise a lot place to move around.

Chapter Four: Happy Household for Your Russian Tortoises

Heat pads

Your Russian Tortoise needs a specific temperature for it to maintain its comfort. A great way to produce warmth for your pet is using heat pads.

You just need to stick the heat pad at the farthest part of the enclosure and leave it there. Constantly check the temperature because a rise in temperature is not really good for your pet. A heat pad could cause you to lessen the need to buy a light.

Typically, the warmest spot of your terrarium is the basking area. It should be around 90 to 95 degrees F. There should be a gradient in the cage to provide the coolest to the warmest spot of the area. You can easily track the monitor through using a thermometer.

Aside from heat pads, you can also use under tank heaters and ceramic emitters. Further, you can use incandescent heat lamps or even infrared bulbs. You can use a variety of these things to suit the size, age, and gender of the Russian Tortoise. A word of caution, do not use any heat rocks for the enclosure.

These are just some things that you need to prepare for your Russian Tortoise's habitat. Do not worry, most of these things are just a one - time expense, you just need to track the usage and make sure that you do not over use it

Chapter Four: Happy Household for Your Russian Tortoises

Habitat Tips

1. In filling up your water bowl, use only non-chlorinated water. For drinking purposes, make sure to give natural spring water. The water should be given and replaced daily.

2. For indoor enclosures, you can use a screen cover with a protective mesh. This would prevent any particles from dropping in the enclosure but still provide you with fresh air.

3. When buying UV light, make sure you get those with timers. These materials would mimic light patterns in your Russian Tortoise's natural environment.

4. You need to have a thermometer to constantly check both the air and water temperature. An imbalance of either of these temperatures would lead to your pet's death.

5. If you are going to use filters, remember that bigger filers are better. Small filters could suck up small particles in the terrarium and would not clean it well.

Chapter Four: Happy Household for Your Russian Tortoises

6. Maintain a regular temperature especially in the basking area. The temperature should only be around 90 to 95 degrees F.

7. Carefully reduce the temperature in the air by 10 degrees during night time.

8. A heat pad is your best friend. Make sure you place it under the tank. This would ensure that the water temperature would tick to 70 degrees F.

9. Set up your terrarium wisely. Make sure there are enough spaces for your pet to move on. You do not want your pet to be stuck in either region.

10. Determine a place where there would be no constant change in temperature.

11. Buy a big terrarium for your pet. You do not want to constantly change your terrarium due to the growing size of your pet.

When giving a habitat for your pet, make sure you give just enough for your pet. Sometimes, you do not know that you are harming your pet with too much light or too much heat in the area.

Chapter Four: Happy Household for Your Russian Tortoises

In this portion, we will give you tips in keeping a healthy terrarium for the pet.

Habitat Maintenance Tips

- Make sure you regularly check and clean your Russian Tortoise's terrarium. See that there are no wastes, rotten food, and other things that would make a filthy environment for your pet.

- Have a standard humidity for the enclosure. Ask your vet on the proper humidity for your pet. Different substrates need different humidity levels.

- Check every spot of the enclosure. Any missed spot could cause a disease for the pet, and worse, even you.

- Remove any uneaten food of your pet. Regularly change the water from the drinking area of your pet. This would make sure that you won't get any unwanted parasites inside.

- If you plan to clean the whole terrarium, make sure to remove the pet and clean everywhere! This would

Chapter Four: Happy Household for Your Russian Tortoises

include the hiding spots, water dishes, and even the substrate.

- When cleaning your tank, make sure you have a cleaning tank where you can safely put your Russian Tortoise.

The Proper Housing Temperature

Just like anyone, your Russian Tortoise needs a specific housing temperature to maintain its comfort.

Outdoor Housing

Any reptile is a cold blooded creature. In this sense, your Russian Tortoise is also a cold blooded animal. Any extreme temperature that is above freezing and below 40.5 Celsius is not great for your pet.

If they reach this extreme temperature, it might experience several difficulties and some might end up dead. The ideal temperature outdoors is 20 to 35 Celsius during the summer and 5 to 10 Celsius during winter.

Chapter Four: Happy Household for Your Russian Tortoises

Indoor Housing

Russian Tortoises are of the Mediterranean species, which means there is a difference in temperature between the day time and night time.

You should set up a housing that has a different temperature. Your Russian Tortoise would move side to side depending to its need.

Hibernation

Your Russian Tortoise undergoes hibernation for months. Usually, the hibernation is a natural mechanism used to protect cold-blooded creatures during cold weather. When your Russian Tortoise is dormant, this would affect the reproductive cycle of the specie.

Your pet could easily hibernate for around 8 months in a year! However, your location greatly affects the hibernation period.

You can easily spot the Russian Tortoise in hibernation mode if you see that it does not really like the temperature it is in. The hibernation period of the Russian Tortoise would be around December and until March of next year.

Chapter Four: Happy Household for Your Russian Tortoises

Before the hibernation period, you need to make sure that the digestive tract of your pet is empty, because the food will rot during this period, worse, your pet might die due to the rotting.

If you are unsure of the hibernation cycle of your pet, you could consult your vet to know more.

Types of Hibernations

A Russian Tortoise could hibernate for as long as eight months per year, while some specie could only hibernate either five months a year or the least eight weeks in captivity.

If they are affected by parasites or even ill, your Russian Tortoise could not undergo hibernation.

Normally, an animal would hibernate inside of something. However, this does not hold true for our beloved Russian Tortoise.

Your Russian Tortoise could hibernate both inside and outside of your house. The difference between the two places is great. In this section, we will discuss them thoroughly.

Chapter Four: Happy Household for Your Russian Tortoises

OUTDOOR HIBERNATION

When your Russian Tortoise hibernates outdoors, you need to give them a stable temperature to work on. An important consideration that these tortoises look for is the temperature that they will be in.

If it is warm enough and there is enough light, your Russian Tortoise could hibernate outside. Your pet could not withstand colder temperature and if they find the temperature unsuitable, they will hibernate indoors.

In these cases, your Russian Tortoise would dig burrows and try to hibernate underground. Your tortoise should have enough time to dig before the cold weather comes.

INDOOR HIBERNATION

In this set-up, your Russian Tortoise would love to be in warmer temperature. The temperature in this environment should be around 68 to 70 degrees.

If they decide to hibernate indoors, they would like an area that contains an overhead light with a temperature between 90 to 100 degrees. This is the main reason why your Russian Tortoise needs UV-B light.

Chapter Four: Happy Household for Your Russian Tortoises

Post - Hibernation

The period and type of hibernation would greatly differ on the place and kind of Russian Tortoise that you would have; although, most Russian Tortoise hibernate during winter season.

Your pet would hibernate if the temperature would suit them properly, so make sure that you could mimic their natural environment into your own home. Smaller specie would have a shorter hibernation period while the adult ones could hibernate for around 3 to 5 months.

In this case, do not give your Russian Tortoise any food two to three weeks before the hibernation period, and make sure to maintain a correct temperature in the area.

These are just some of the primary things to prepare before the arrival of your pet. Make sure you have more than enough supplies to make your pets stay cozy.

Aside from that, determine whether you will build an indoor or outdoor habitat and set aside a specific place for your pet to stay in.

Chapter Four: Happy Household for Your Russian Tortoises

Chapter Five: Russian Tortoise's Feeding Guide

Food is an important aspect in anybody's life. However, you must thoroughly know the specie before giving it something to eat.

If you do not give the correct food for your pet, you might compromise its health, lead to diseases, and sometimes might even end up in death. So make sure that you know what your Russian Tortoise eats and how much.

This chapter will give you a thorough nutritional guideline for your pet. We have also included some feeding tips to ensure that your pet will be eating right and having the correct nutrients in its body.

Chapter Five: Russian Tortoise's Feeding Guide

A Suitable Diet for My Russian Tortoise

Diet is one of the most important factors in keeping your Russian Tortoise's health. Among the top ten lists of important things, food and UV exposure are the top two things.

Providing food for your Russian Tortoise is very easy, providing that you know what kind of food to give your pet. Luckily, the foods that they eat are just simple and straightforward. There is no mystery or specific recipe, and you do not need to maintain it way too much.

Your Russian Tortoise needs a diet with high fiber but low in protein. Where could your find this? In plants! There are a lot of plant matters that you can give to your pet; however, not all plants should be given to your pet.

One of the best diets that you can give to your pet is a variety of weeds (flowers and leaves); Russian Tortoises favourite food is the Dandelion.

If there are good foods for your pets, there are also "anti-nutrients" for your pet. If you have given these things, this would lead to poor health. Some anti-nutrients are oxalic acid, goitrogens, tannins, phytic acid, and purines. In the succeeding portions, you will get to know these more.

Remember, your Russian Tortoise is programmed to eat a lot in a certain period of time. In the wilderness, they

Chapter Five: Russian Tortoise's Feeding Guide

are only active for a few times in a year. After their hibernation, they will eat a lot in preparation for their aestivation, a summer hibernation, or as other people would call it…"a long siesta",

In captivity, they are almost active throughout the year; this case would give them the chance to eat easily. If you have kept them in an indoor enclosure, they would only get lesser exercise than in the wild. These two things could potentially lead to a shortened life span and a rapid growth. In this case, you should give a healthy yet restricted diet to your pet.

When they are staying outdoors, they could freely run around and could be fed daily in small amounts plus any other supplemental food. You could plant some weeds and flowers for your Russian Tortoise.

If you plan to let them stay indoors, they would have lesser exercise and would just rely on greens that are usually bought from the grocery. In this case, it is best to feed them for only a certain number of minutes per day, or an hour, but in this case, only every other day.

You could also chop up hay, such as bermuda, orchard, or timothy, and mix it with several greens which you can feed your Russian Tortoise. You could also leave fresh hay in the enclosure all day.

Chapter Five: Russian Tortoise's Feeding Guide

Variation Is the Key

When personalizing a healthy diet for your Russian Tortoise, you can create a variety. You should mix flowers and plants at every meal. Both of these things are easy to find and you would not have a trouble giving a variety of things for your Russian Tortoise. However, remember that green should be the base of this diet even if your give a variety of food within the week.

The Good Stuff

In this section, we will be giving you a wide array of food choices, supplements, and vitamins which you can freely give your Russian Tortoise.

GREENS

Greens are nature's gift not only to humans but also animals. In most grocery stores, you can find a lot of selection of greens that your Russian Tortoise would love to eat.

Ideally, you should only give greens that are both organic and pesticide free; but in the real world, you can't really find these ideal food.

In the succeeding parts, we will give you a list of foods that you can give to your pet. As we have said, you

Chapter Five: Russian Tortoise's Feeding Guide

should give a variety of these things to your pet. Do not give them the same food that you have given in the day and at night.

Food You Can Give To Your Russian Tortoise

In the wilderness, the Russian Tortoise likes to hibernate from October until March. In this essence, they are only active for a few months in a year. They like to hibernate when the weather is not that favorable to them.

When they are native Russian Tortoise, you should only give them a massive amount of the proper food so they could have enough food that would last through their hibernation.

If you a Russian Tortoise as a pet, these are some of the things that you can give them in captivity:

- Grasses
- Alfalfa
- Clover
- Hibiscus (the leaves and the flowers)
- Red leaf lettuce
- Kale
- Rose petals (if no pesticides were used on them)
- Turnip greens
- Mustard greens
- Radicchio
- Dandelions (Russian tortoises

Chapter Five: Russian Tortoise's Feeding Guide

really seem to enjoy dandelion)

- Dandelion
- Endive
- Romaine lettuce
- Mustard greens
- Radicchio
- Spring mix
- Chicory
- Collards greens
- Kale
- Finely chopped hay
- Rose flowers that are pesticide-free
- Mulberry leaves
- Hibiscus flowers
- Prickly pear flowers
- Fruit in moderation
- Plantain weed
- Cornflowers
- Mallow flowers
- Chrysanthemum flowers
- Californian poppy
- Chia
- Forsythia
- Day-flower
- Spinach only in moderation
- Adequate fresh water supply
- Ice Plants
- Henbit
- Hosta
- Sedum
- Calcium supplement added to food lightly
- Probiotic supplement IFlora
- Hibiscus (flowers and leaves)
- Hosta

Chapter Five: Russian Tortoise's Feeding Guide

- Sedum
- Hen and Chicks
- Prickly pear flowers, fruit and pads (burn the spines off)
- Plantain (not the banana type fruit....the weed plantago major)
- Mallow (flowers and leaves)
- Henbit
- Chrysanthemum flowers
- Californian Poppy
- Cornflowers
- Forsythia
- Dayflower

The Bad Stuff

If there is good stuff, there is also bad stuff that you should not give to your Russian Tortoise. Any human food, except for those that are listed as good pellet type food should not be given to your pet.

Some of the foods that you should not give are the ones that contain wheat, soy, or rice. These foods contain high omega 6 fatty acids that would have a negative effect on the health of your Russian Tortoise. These foods would cause leaching of the bones. Other than that, these are also high in phytate which binds calcium with other minerals. Grains would alter the effects of Vitamin D.

Chapter Five: Russian Tortoise's Feeding Guide

Diets high in grains have a negative effect on bone growth, even though your pet has enough exposure to sunlight.

Anti - Nutrients

There are a number of food items that have chemicals that interferes with the tortoise's ability to absorb the mineral from the food that they are eating.

Although most of these things are commonly found in food, a variety of these things in a diet could minimize the effects.

Oxalic Acid

Oxalic Acid is a naturally occurring element in many plants. This acid gives of a bitter taste in greens, such as mustard green. Aside from this, this binds minerals; a great example would be calcium. This must be eliminated through the kidneys.

If given in large amounts, or small quantities with improper hydration, this would lead to kidney stones and kidney damage. Do not give rhubarb and beet green and limit spinach in the diet.

Chapter Five: Russian Tortoise's Feeding Guide

Phytic Acid

This acid is found in large number in peas, cereals, and beans. This chemical binds minerals as well as the proteins.

Tannins

For the most part, Tannis is very beneficial. However, if ingested in large quantities, just like any other anti-nutrients, this would bind protein and would interfere with proper digestion.

Purines

This is well known to humans as a great contributing factor in gout. If your Russian Tortoise has eaten a large amount, this would lead to kidney disease.

Goitrogens

This compound is a great factor in the development of enlarged thyroid glands, also known as goiters. This interferes with the uptake of iodine.

Chapter Five: Russian Tortoise's Feeding Guide

What Not To Give To My Russian Tortoise:

- Iceberg lettuce
- Bok Choy
- Dog and cat food
- Any type of grains (breads, pasta, oats, etc.)
- Meat
- wild cherry
- black cherry
- trumpet flower
- sweet pea
- Nightshade
- morning glory,
- lily of the valley
- Jerusalem cherry,
- English ivy
- golden-seal
- Foxglove
- belladonna,
- China-berry
- castor-bean
- butterfly-weed
- burning bush
- spindle tree
- bleeding heart
- bane-berry
- Amaryllis
- Boxwood
- Azalea

There are many other dangerous plants that you should not give your Russian Tortoise. If you are unable to recognize the plant matter that you will be giving to your pet Russian Tortoise, it is best to consult an expert. If you have given these or any other dangerous plants to your pet

Chapter Five: Russian Tortoise's Feeding Guide

Russian Tortoise, it would get diseases, illnesses, and even death. Be careful in choosing the food that you will give to your pet.

Supplements: Yay or Nay?

Do I need to add anything else to my Russian Tortoise's diet? Is the food I have given him enough to give all the vitamins and minerals he needs? Do I need to add calcium or any other supplements in creating my Russian Tortoise's diet?

These are just some of the questions you need to answer when preparing a curated diet for your Russian Tortoise. All of these maybe difficult questions to be answered by first time reptile owners. But, if you give your pet a great habitat and diet, you would not really need to give supplements.

If you already gave your tortoise a high variety of diet with plenty of high calcium greens, plus a hefty exposure to sunlight then you would not really need to supplement its diet at all. However, if you are keeping your Russian Tortoise at home where it does not receive any natural sunlight, you might need to supplement calcium on its diet.

You can give high calcium greens and cuttlebone to your Russian Tortoise. In this way, your pet would have its own calcium intake. Cuttlebone is steered away from the

Chapter Five: Russian Tortoise's Feeding Guide

conversation, but this is needed when females or young tortoise is experiencing a growth sprout.

Some high calcium plants are collard greens, kale, mustard greens, and turnip greens.

Cuttlebone is the bony internal structure inside of a cuttlefish. This is given as a calcium-rich dietary supplement for different animals such as tortoises and turtles. You can easily buy it in pet stores and even online shops.

Where Can I Buy Food For My Russian Tortoise?

First time owners are really scared and nervous as to where they could find the best food for their Russian Tortoise. This list will provide you with places you can buy the food for an excellent diet:

Grocery Stores

This is the common choice for many pet owners as they do not have enough time to go out and collect food in the wild. Good thing is that some of the diet foods needed by the Russian Tortoise can be easily found in the grocery store.

Some of the foods are romaine lettuce, mustard green, turnip greens, collard, endive, radicchio, spring mix, kale, and chicory. Other foods that you can buy from the grocery

Chapter Five: Russian Tortoise's Feeding Guide

store are spinach, Probiotic supplement, fruit, and calcium supplement.

Online Shops

If you're planning to own a Russian Tortoise, you can save all the trouble from the traditional grocery shopping and just buy online a few foods for their diet.

A good thing for that online shop is that they ship these items directly at home which will save you a lot of time and energy in choosing and carrying the stuff.

However, only some of these things are on sale. Some foods that you can purchase are probiotic supplement and calcium supplement.

Your Russian Tortoise would reward you so much if you take care and give it a healthy and well-balanced diet. You should thoroughly see the reviews of the sites as well as be informed and make great shopping purchases when shopping online.

You can buy dried flowers and herbs from health food stores or herbal supply stores. Remember, dried Dandelions make the best healthy snack for your Russian Tortoise.

Chapter Five: Russian Tortoise's Feeding Guide

Pet Stores

You can typically buy your Russian Tortoise from the pet stores. Logically, these pet stores would also include tortoise pellet diets, timothy hay, wheat grass, orchard grass, and the Bermuda Grass. However, you still need to check the labels closely to see if it has high quality ingredients. Your local pet stores would also have a high supply of calcium supplement with added phosphorus.

You need to contact your Russian Tortoise to see if you are getting a good advice in buying healthy Russian Tortoise diet.

Grow Food by Yourself

If you have a green thumb, you can surely save money by growing your pet Russian Tortoise's own food. A good thing about this method is that you will have a fresh and nice supply of food on hand when you need to feed the pet.

However, farming will be time consuming; but this will send a note of love for your Russian Tortoise. Some foods that you can grow by yourself are dandelion flowers, some fruit, broad leafy greens, roses, mallow flowers, cornflowers, and spinach.

Chapter Five: Russian Tortoise's Feeding Guide

Local Farmer's Market

Your local farmer's market carry a lot of fresh supply of leafy greens that your pet Russian Tortoise would enjoy eating. If you are planning a trip to your local farmer's market, you must purchase food like lettuce, spinach, fruit, kale, spring mix, and chicory.

Water

Water is important to almost all living things. This holds true for our dearest animal, and your Russian Tortoise is not an exception to this rule.

Because Russian Tortoises are arid creatures, most of the water is extracted from the food that they ate. In whatever way possible, you should give a regular source.

You can put a shallow bowl of water inside their enclosures. If they are staying indoors, you need to soak them in cheap deep warm water for 20 minutes every two to three days. This technique serves two purposes; it will allow you to inspect your pet frequently and this will get their cages much cleaner.

If you know how to properly take care of your pet Russian Tortoise, it will live a happy, long, and healthy life. Feeding it a healthy well balanced diet would give it proper nutrients and vitamins for their body.

Chapter Five: Russian Tortoise's Feeding Guide

You need to plan to give it a healthy diet combined with an active healthy exercise plan for your pet, and you will see that your pet is trying hard to maintain its shape.

Your Russian Tortoise needs a high - fiber diet rich in minerals and vitamins to keep it very healthy from ailments, illnesses, and diseases.

If you have gotten your Russian Tortoise from the wild, you need to have it checked with the vet first, to know if the specie is right for you and if it is overall healthy. When you take your pet at home, you need to provide an environment that would mimic its natural habitat. You can add hay and sand to the substrate to make it feel at home.

Your Russian Tortoise would bring much joy into your life and your family and friends if you properly take care of it.

Chapter Six: Proper Hygiene and Grooming For Your Russian Tortoise

Hygiene is an important aspect of the life of your Russian Tortoise. You should know that hygiene is a keen element so your pet Russian Tortoise would have a happy, healthy, and long life.

If you fail to provide proper hygiene and grooming for your pet, it would potentially lead to parasites, infections, or worse, death. You should learn these things as you will be the one to bathe and groom your own pet.

In this chapter, we will give you a rundown on the basic grooming and hygiene techniques for your Russian Tortoise.

Chapter Six: Proper Hygiene and Grooming

Hygiene for Your Russian Tortoise

An important detail that you need to always remember is to wash your hands with antibacterial soap with lukewarm water. Do this before and after you handle, groom, and bathe your Russian Tortoise. If you do this, you and your pet will benefit from this task.

Grooming 101

The nails and beak of your Russian Tortoise will lengthen, so you need to trim it religiously. Your Russian Tortoise's nails and beak grow long because it is staying in the places with soft substrate. To prevent the lengthening of the nails and beak, you should only give rough substrate and put rocks for your Russian Tortoise to hide and crawl on. If you put a flat rock on the substrate, your Russian Tortoise could use this as a tasty treat.

If you just let your pet have long nails and beak, this would probably lead to a Metabolic Bone Disease (MBD). MBD is from an imbalance of calcium and phosphorus in your Russian Tortoise's diet. To prevent this from happening, you need to use a nail file or an emery board to trim and file the nail and the beak.

Doing this task more often will make you and your pet more comfortable. You need to file the nails in which the nail is growing. A great food to put in the substrate for your

Chapter Six: Proper Hygiene and Grooming

Russian Tortoise to chew on is cuttlebones and hard vegetable such as carrots. These things will help your Russian Tortoise trim its beak.

In extreme and rare cases, you can use a bird or dog nail trimmers. You should not trim the nail or beak too far. In order for you to see the vein, hold the nail up near a light, other than that, be careful when cutting the Russian Tortoise' beak. You might damage the beak if you do not cut it properly.

You can contact your vet for his recommendation if you do not know where to cut the nails and the beak. You may even let the vet trim the nails for a while and see how he does it. However, if you think this is an easy task, you can do it by yourself.

Russian Tortoise is commonly known as Horsefield Tortoise. This specie lives in dry places. In general, they thrive in warmer, low humidity environments.

In this kind of habitat, they are in great danger of being dehydrated. Aside from this, your Russian Tortoise could have a dirt build up in its skin and shells. To prevent this phenomenon, you need to regularly clean your Russian Tortoise.

Bathing your Russian Tortoise would make them hydrated, clean, and groomed. Your vet would recommend you bath your adult once a week, but a hatchling on a daily basis. Before you do this task, you need to have all the materials ready, wash your Russian Tortoise, and cleanse you and Russian Tortoise carefully when you are finished with your task.

Prepare the Materials:

Step #1: Prepare a big tray or a shallow container. This basin should be big enough to suit your Russian Tortoise. Realistically, when you choose a container, it should be made of either porcelain or a cloudy plastic container. If you choose either of these, you would not lure your pet to climb out of the container. Aside from this, you can also use a baking dish that is made of large porcelain or a kitty litter pan but it should only be shallow. However, if you determine which kind of container to use, make sure that you only need it for bathing purposes. If you have already used the container to bathe your pet, this container will not be suitable anymore for food preparation or any other specific purpose.

Step #2: Have all your supplies on hand. Have all the supplies ready in a pan, cup, or even as small can. These supplies would help you to rinse your Russian Tortoise. If you ever clean your pet, make sure you only utilize a nail brush or even a soft

Chapter Six: Proper Hygiene and Grooming

bristle brush. Aside from that, you need to paper a roll of towels.

Step #3: Add lukewarm water to the bathing pan.
Remember to add lukewarm, clean water into the pan. Put the water slowly starting from the bottom part of the container. However, make sure that the water would only reach the bottom part of the shell of the Russian Tortoise. Aside from that, the water should only be lukewarm. Hot water could potentially harm your pet. Do not add any other soap, detergents, or any products into the water because it might hurt them.

Step #4: Put a small item under the container to tilt it. Put a small book or a similarly sized object that would tilt the container of your Russian Tortoise. When you put this object, there would be two environments created; a deep and shallow end. Place only the head of your Russian Tortoise on the shallow part, while its rear on the deep part of the container.

Chapter Six: Proper Hygiene and Grooming
Cleaning Your Russian Tortoise Thoroughly

Step #1: Clean your hands thoroughly with lukewarm water and an anti-bacterial soap. You need to secure both you and your Russian Tortoise's health. Make sure that your hands are cleansed before you handled any bathing materials or your pet Russian Tortoise.

Step #2: Place your pet Russian Tortoise in the bathing pan. Slowly lower your pet Russian Tortoise into the bathing container. Let your pet Russian Tortoise settle into the water before you do any bathing procedure. Do not forcefully place your Russian Tortoise into the water.

Step #3: Submerge your pet Russian Tortoise around 10 to a half an hour. Let your pet Russian Tortoise soak in lukewarm water. When you do this activity, this would moisten your Russian Tortoise's skin, let your pet Russian Tortoise drink, and for it to eliminate its body waste. However, do not put too much cold water into the container as your Russian Tortoise needs the head from its neighboring environment to function well. Remove a small part of the water from time to time and put lukewarm water in between the task. Aside from this, always be there for

Chapter Six: Proper Hygiene and Grooming

your Russian Tortoise. If you leave your pet Russian Tortoise alone, it might overturn and drown easily.

Step #4: Let a small amount of lukewarm water flow over your pet Russian Tortoise. Prepare a separate pan when rinsing your pet Russian Tortoise's limb, shell, and head. When you do this thing, this would remove any dirt and debris as well as moisten the parts of the Russian Tortoise that are not put into the bathing container. Pour a small amount of water to your pet Russian Tortoise; you may even use a small watering can to mimic a shower head.

Step #5: Prepare a soft-bristled and small tooth brush. You will use this to scrub your Russian Tortoise's shell. When all the dirt has already been softened, you could possibly scrub any other debris left with a soft brush and a small amount of lukewarm water. Scrub the left over dirt and debris with your brush and water. After rinsing everything from your Russian Tortoise's body, make sure you remove and rinse the dirt and debris that might get trapped in the brush by letting running water go through it. When scrubbing your pet, give close attention between the scutes and the upper shell. You could also rub the limb, tail, and head because some debris could build up in these places.

Step #6: Rub and rinse your pet Russian Tortoise's neck, limbs, and tail. Put a gentle hand when you are cleaning these parts of your pet Russian Tortoise. These areas do not have scales and your pet might get hurt in this process.

Step #7: Inspect and check all the injuries, problems, and any other things. Scrutinize your pet Russian Tortoise for injuries, shell damage, signs of Stomatitis, or any other problem that might be a threat for your pet Russian Tortoise. Make sure that you contact your pet immediately if you notice some irregularities in your pet Russian Tortoise. Study for anything related to injuries, infections, or red spots around its beak and mouth. These small spots could be a big sign of stomatitis or mouth rot. Any signs of shell discoloration, lesions, or cracks could be a big problem for your and your pet Russian Tortoise. Also see if there are mites around the head and limbs which may look like red or black dots. You can remove it using a soft bristled tooth brush and with running water.

Step #8: Dab your pet Russian Tortoise with paper towels. After the bathing process of your pet Russian Tortoise, make sure you gently pat down your Russian Tortoise's head, limbs, and shell before you return it to its enclosure. Make sure that your pet is thoroughly dry to prevent any problems especially with its shell that would be caused by excessive humidity. After rubbing down your pet, dispose of any materials

Chapter Six: Proper Hygiene and Grooming

immediately. Put these things in closed garbage to prevent any spread disease and parasites.

Step #9: Cleans all the container and make sure to remove the bath water in it. Put the bath water straight into the toilet to protect you and your family. Clean the container with hot water and mild detergent. Remember to scrub all parts of the tub thoroughly.

Step #10: Rub and wash both of your hands with soap and warm water (again). After bathing and grooming your pet Russian Tortoise, you need to wash both of your hands again. This would stop the spread of salmonella and other disease that might be transmittable to human.

These are just some basic things that you need to remember when grooming your pet. Remember, providing a great hygiene practice for your pet is essential to make sure that it will have a happy and healthy life

Chapter Six: Proper Hygiene and Grooming

Chapter Seven: Care Sheet and Summary

We have thoroughly discussed about the world of the Russian Tortoise. We have given you in detail about its wonderful history, known facts, as well as feeding guidelines for your pet.

We wish that it would have made up your mind that you will get a Russian Tortoise now. However, make sure that you are ready with all the materials for your pet.

In this chapter, we will summarize everything that we have learned from the past couple of chapters.

Chapter Seven: Care Sheet and Summary

The Russian Tortoise

Costs of Owning a Russian Tortoise:

- **Purchase Price:** A hatchling's price could shoot up to $225. An adult female could be priced up $149 to $249.

- **Bedding and Substrate:** You need to have a bedding material that will serve as your tortoise's footing and temperature regulation. This will cost anywhere from $20 to $30 per bag or more.

- **Lighting/ Heating Equipment:** UV-B bulbs are typically $20 up to $40, while UV-A bulbs range from $10 to $20.

- **Terrarium:** A room for one or two adults should be more than 2 feet by 4 feet. The walls should be around six to 12 inches from the ground; this is to prevent your tortoise to dig from the side. Aside from it, it should be 12 inches or higher above the ground. The total cost is around $200

- **Filter System and Pump:** A good filter system starts at $70.

Chapter Seven: Care Sheet and Summary

- **Food per month:** Your Russian Tortoise is herbivores in their nature. The diet should have a variety of leafy, dark, greens. Aside from this, you could also add squash, carrots, and bell peppers. You could also give figs, bananas, apple, and strawberries, but only as a treat. Typically, your budget would run from $45 and up.

- **Veterinary Needs:** Make sure to set aside a budget of around $50 and up for any medical needs.

Reputable Breeder Finder

Seek advice. Ask your friends, relatives, and family members if they know any Russian Tortoise breeder.

Research. Join online forums and talk to other reptile enthusiasts and ask for their opinion.

Further research. Seek for sites about Russian Tortoise.

Weed out the bad stuff. If the website does not offer enough information that you need, just like the specie, breed, or facilities, cross it off your list.

Fact Check. Make sure that you check the accuracy of the data and the website itself.

Chapter Seven: Care Sheet and Summary

Cross it off! If the breeder does not answer your questions in the way that you want, cross it off.

Watch out for Red Flags. If you see that the breeding facility is dirty, cramped up with too much Russian Tortoise - remove it from your list!

Have human interaction. You need to contact each breeder individually.

Answer back. A reputable breeder would also ask you questions about yourself.

Give it time. Allot time to going through every detail. Although it might be tiring, you will be ensured that the tortoise you would be getting is of great quality.

Tortoise Health Checklist

- ✓ Your tortoise should have clear eyes, clean nose, and clean bum.
- ✓ There should not be any signs of shell damage.
- ✓ The Russian Tortoise should be active or alert at all times.
- ✓ The tortoise should feel strong and heavy.

Chapter Seven: Care Sheet and Summary

Tortoise Health Red Flags:

There are things that you still need to avoid, such as:

- Cloudy eyes
- There is a mucus build - up in the nose
- There is a residue on the bum
- There is a visual damage on the shell, or "pyramiding"
- The tortoise is incoherent or non-responsive
- If you feel that the Russian Tortoise is weak or light.
- If the breeding area is too crowded with different kinds of tortoises.

Husbandry Tips

- In filling up your water bowl, use only non-chlorinated water
- For indoor enclosures, you can use a screen cover with a protective mesh.
- When buying UV light, make sure you get those with timers.
- You need to have a thermometer to constantly check both the air and water temperature.
- If you are going to use filters, remember that bigger filers are better.

Chapter Seven: Care Sheet and Summary

- Maintain a regular temperature especially in the basking area.
- Carefully reduce the temperature in the air by 10 degrees during night time.
- A heat pad is your best friend. Make sure you place it under the tank.
- Set up your terrarium wisely. Make sure there are enough spaces for your pet to move on.
- Determine a place where there would be no constant change in temperature.
- Buy a big terrarium for your pet.

Food Sources for Tortoises

Grocery Stores

Some of the foods are romaine lettuce, mustard green, turnip greens, collard, endive, radicchio, spring mix, kale, and chicory. Other foods that you can buy from the grocery store are spinach, Probiotic supplement, fruit, and calcium supplement.

Chapter Seven: Care Sheet and Summary

Online Stores

Some foods that you can purchase are probiotic supplement and calcium supplement. You can buy dried flowers and herbs from health food stores or herbal supply online stores.

Pet Stores

Pet stores offer various tortoise diets such as tortoise pellet diets, timothy hay, wheat grass, orchard grass, and the Bermuda Grass.

Local Farmer's Market

If you are planning a trip to your local farmer's market, you must purchase food like lettuce, spinach, fruit, kale, spring mix, and chicory.

Organic Plants

Some foods that you can grow by yourself are dandelion flowers, some fruit, broad leafy greens, roses, mallow flowers, cornflowers, and spinach.

Chapter Seven: Care Sheet and Summary

Grooming Your Pet Tortoise

Preparation Tips

- When choosing a container, it should be made of either porcelain or a cloudy plastic container. If you choose either of these, you would not lure your pet to climb out of the container.

- Have all the supplies ready in a pan, cup, or even as small can. These supplies would help you to rinse your Russian Tortoise.

- Remember to add lukewarm, clean water into the pan. Put the water slowly starting from the bottom part of the container.

- Put a small book or a similarly sized object that would tilt the container of your Russian Tortoise.

Grooming Proper

- You need to secure both you and your Russian Tortoise's health. Make sure that your hands are cleansed before you handled any bathing materials

Chapter Seven: Care Sheet and Summary

- Slowly lower your pet Russian Tortoise into the bathing container. Let your pet Russian Tortoise settle into the water before you do any bathing procedure.

- Let your pet Russian Tortoise soak in lukewarm water. When you do this activity, this would moisten your Russian Tortoise's skin, let your pet Russian Tortoise drink, and for it to eliminate its body waste.

- Prepare a separate pan when rinsing your pet Russian Tortoise's limb, shell, and head.

- When all the dirt has already been softened, you could possibly scrub any other debris left with a soft brush and a small amount of lukewarm water. When scrubbing your pet, give close attention between the scutes and the upper shell. You could also rub the limb, tail, and head because some debris could build up in these places.

- Put a gentle hand when you are cleaning these parts of your pet Russian Tortoise.

- Scrutinize your pet Russian Tortoise for injuries, shell damage, signs of Stomatitis, or any other problem that might be a threat for your pet Russian Tortoise.

Chapter Seven: Care Sheet and Summary

- After the bathing process of your pet Russian Tortoise, make sure you gently pat down your Russian Tortoise's head, limbs, and shell before you return it to its enclosure.

- Put the bath water straight into the toilet to protect you and your family. Remember to scrub all parts of the tub thoroughly.

- After bathing and grooming your pet Russian Tortoise, you need to wash both of your hands again.

This book has helped you a lot to gain new information and knowledge about the Russian Tortoise. Remember, thoroughly commit to the task to have a happy and healthy relationship with your pet!

Glossary

Acclimation – Adjusting to a new environment or new conditions over a period of time

Acrylic Aquarium – Glass aquarium alternative, usually lighter than an ordinary aquarium but can be easily scratched.

Active range – The area of activity which can include hunting, seeking refuge, and finding a mate

Ambient temperature – The overall temperature of the environment

Amelanistic – Amel for short; without melanin, or without any black or brown coloration.

Ammonia – made up of nitrogen and hydrogen. It has an unpleasant smell that's also toxic and corrosive. Leftover food in the enclosure can be contributing factors that build up ammonia

Anerythristic – Anery for short; without any red coloration.

Aquatic – Lives in water.

Arboreal – Lives in trees.

Bacteria – microorganisms that are distributed widely in the environments. Tortoise keepers should be aware of the harmful effects of bacteria

Bacteria Bloom – sometimes referred to as a tank syndrome.

Basking – a procedure where tortoises or turtles warms or dries up their body. Tortoises will need to have a basking area at a certain temperature to prevent shell rot. It also allows absorption of UVA and UVB for thermoregulation

Betadine – An antiseptic that can be used to clean wounds in reptiles

Bilateral – Where stripes, spots or markings are present on both sides of an animal.

Biotic – The living components of an environment.

Bridge – part of the shell that's located in the middle of the front and black legs connecting the top and bottom shell.

Brumation – The equivalent of mammalian hibernation among reptiles

Cannibalistic – Where an animal feeds on others of its own kind.

Cloaca – also vent; a half-moon shaped opening for digestive waste disposal and sexual organs.

Cloacal Gaping – Indication of sexual receptivity of the female.

Cloacal Gland – A gland at the base of the tail which emits foul smelling liquid as a defense mechanism; also called Anal Gland.

Clutch – A batch of eggs.

Constriction – The act of wrapping or coiling around a prey to subdue and kill it prior to eating.

Crepuscular – Active at twilight, usually from dusk to dawn.

Diurnal – Active by day

Drop – To lay eggs or to bear live young

Ectothermic – Cold-blooded. An animal that cannot regulate its own body temperature, but sources body heat from the surroundings

Endemic – Indigenous to a specific region or area.

Estivation – Also Aestivation; a period of dormancy that usually occurs during the hot or dry seasons in order to escape the heat or to remain hydrated.

Flexarium – A reptile enclosure that is mostly made from mesh screening, for species that require plenty of ventilation.

Fossorial – A burrowing species.

Gestation – The period of development of an embryo within a female.

Gravid – The equivalent of pregnant in reptiles

Gut-loading – Feeding insects within 24 hours to a prey before they are fed to your pet, so that they pass on the nutritional benefits

Hatchling – A newly hatched, or baby, reptile.

Herps/Herpetiles – A collective name for reptile and amphibian species.

Herpetoculturist – A person who keeps and breeds reptiles in captivity

Herpetologist – A person who studies ectothermic animals, sometimes also used for those who keeps reptiles.

Herpetology – The study of reptiles and amphibians.

Hide Box – A furnishing within a reptile cage that gives the animal a secure place to hide.

Husbandry – The daily care of a pet reptile.

Hygrometer – Used to measure humidity.

Impaction – A blockage in the digestive tract due to the swallowing of an object that cannot be digested or broken down.

Incubate – Maintaining eggs in conditions favorable for development and hatching.

Juvenile – Not yet adult; not of breedable age

LTC – Long Term Captive; or one that has been in captivity for more than six months.

MBD – Metabolic Bone Disease; occurs when reptiles lack sufficient calcium in their diet.

Morph – Color pattern

Musking – Secretion of a foul smelling liquid from its vent as a defense mechanism.

Oviparous – Egg-bearing.

Ovoviviparous – Eggs are retained inside the female's body until they hatch.

Popping – The process by which the sex is determined among hatchlings.

Probing – The process by which the sex is determined among adults.

Sloughing – Shedding.

Sub-adult – Juvenile

Substrate – The material lining the bottom of a reptile enclosure.

Stat – Short for Thermostat

Tag – Slang for a bite or being bitten

Terrarium – A reptile enclosure.

Thermo-regulation – The process by which cold-blooded animals regulate their body temperature by moving from hot to cold surroundings.

Vent – Cloaca

Vivarium – Glass-fronted enclosure

Viviparous – Gives birth to live young.

WC – Wild Caught

WF – Wild Farmed; refers to the collection of a pregnant female whose eggs or young were hatched or born in captivity.

Yearling – A year old.

Zoonosis – A disease that can be passed from animal to man.

Photo Credits

Page 1 Photo by user Mikey Lemoi via Flickr.com,

https://www.flickr.com/photos/mikeylemoi/6857925551/

Page 4 Photo by user beautifulcataya via Flickr.com,

https://www.flickr.com/photos/beautifulcataya/3873083336/

Page 13 Photo by user Sergey Yeliseev via Flickr.com,

https://www.flickr.com/photos/yeliseev/6192276802/

Page 28 Photo by user Stuart R Brown via Flickr.com,

https://www.flickr.com/photos/edesign/2597811720/

Page 40 Photo by user margaretglin via Flickr.com,

https://www.flickr.com/photos/margaretglin/6974056501/

Page 68 Photo by user Slave2TehTink via Flickr.com,

https://www.flickr.com/photos/slave2tehtink/2703840730/

Page 84 Photo by user Raita Futo via Flickr.com,

https://www.flickr.com/photos/raita/23440024204/

Page 93 Photo by user Heartlover1717 via Flickr.com,

https://www.flickr.com/photos/heartlover1717/4986359360

References

"Russian Tortoise Facts: Anatomy, Diet, Habitat, Behavior" – AnimalsTime.com

http://animalstime.com/russian-tortoise-facts/

"Is a tortoise pet easy or hard to take care of?" – HorsefieldTortoise.co.uk

http://www.horsefieldtortoise.co.uk/is-a-tortoise-pet-easy-or-hard-to-take-care-of/

"12 Reasons Not to Buy a Pet Turtle or Tortoise" – PetHelpful.com

https://pethelpful.com/reptiles-amphibians/10-Reason-Not-To-Buy-A-Pet-Turtle-Or-Tortoise

"Is The Russian Tortoise Right For Me?" – Russian-Tortoise.com

http://russian-tortoise.com/is-the-russian-tortoise-right-for-me/

"Russian Tortoise Care Sheet" – ReptilesMagazine.com

http://www.reptilesmagazine.com/Care-Sheets/Russian-Tortoise/

"Russian Tortoise Substrate and Bedding" - Russian – Tortoise.com

http://russian-tortoise.com/russian-tortoise-substrate-and-bedding/

"Considerations for Outdoor Housing of Tortoises" – LLLReptile.com

https://www.lllreptile.com/articles/156-considerations-for-outdoor-housing-of-tortoises/

"Russian Tortoise Substrate and Bedding" - HorsefieldTortoise.co.uk

http://www.horsefieldtortoise.co.uk/russian-tortoise/substrate-and-bedding/

"Russian Tortoise Hibernation Guide" - Russian – Tortoise.com http://russian-tortoise.com/hibernation-guide/#Hibernation

"Russian Tortoise Diet" - RussianTortoise.net

http://www.russiantortoise.net/russiantortoisediet.htm

"Russian Tortoise Diet" - Reptileknowledge.com

http://www.reptileknowledge.com/care/russian-tortoise.php

"Russian Tortoise Food Guide" - Russian – Tortoise.com

http://russian-tortoise.com/food-guide/

"Horsefield tortoise Hygiene, Grooming, Soft Shell and Pyramiding" - Horsefieldtortoise.co.uk

http://www.horsefieldtortoise.co.uk/horsefield-tortoise-hygiene-grooming-soft-shell-and-pyramiding/#Grooming

"Russian Tortoise Illnesses" – Animals.Mom.me

https://animals.mom.me/russian-tortoise-illnesses-4848.html

"Common Health Problems with Russian Tortoises" – Pethelpful.com https://pethelpful.com/reptiles-amphibians/Russian-Tortoises-Health

www.ingramcontent.com/pod-product-compliance
Lightning Source LLC
Chambersburg PA
CBHW060841050426
42453CB00008B/779